GRRR-
ATITUDE

A GUIDED JOURNAL
FOR THE
RELUCTANTLY POSITIVE

April J. Graham

THUNDER BAY
P · R · E · S · S
San Diego, California

Thunder Bay Press
An imprint of Printers Row Publishing Group
10350 Barnes Canyon Road, Suite 100
San Diego, CA 92121
www.thunderbaybooks.com • mail@thunderbaybooks.com

Printers Row Publishing Group is a division of Readerlink Distribution
Services, LLC. Thunder Bay Press is a registered trademark of
Readerlink Distribution Services, LLC.

Correspondence regarding the content of this book should
be addressed to Thunder Bay Press, Editorial Department,
at the above address.

Publisher: Peter Norton
Associate Publisher: Ana Parker
Senior Developmental Editor: April Graham Farr
Designer: Rosemary Rae
Senior Product Manager: Kathryn C. Dalby
Production Team: Jonathan Lopes, Rusty von Dyl

ISBN: 978-1-64517-003-7

Printed in China

23 22 21 20 19 1 2 3 4 5

THIS
JOURNAL
AND THIS
ATTITUDE
BELONG TO

What's the big deal about GRATITUDE, anyway?

Everywhere you look these days, people are talking about gratitude. Books, podcasts, celebrities, that basic b*tch you went to high school with who's always posting "inspirational" crap on Instagram—suddenly, everybody's bragging about how much **#gratitude** they have and how **#blessed** they are. It's super annoying, amirite? Not everybody has a sunny disposition. And some people aren't simply inclined toward negativity, but *enjoy* their negativity. So why the hell should we jump on this gratitude bandwagon?

Unfortunately for you, grumpy pants, it turns out gratitude is good for you. Like, *really* good for you. Gratitude makes you happier, healthier, more self-confident, and less stressed. It makes you more successful at work and makes people like you more. It even helps you sleep better and get fewer colds!

Given all those benefits, you'd be kind of crazy if you didn't at least *try* to be a little more grateful. We get it—it's not easy to be positive or happy. You're stressed, you're tired, your boss is demanding, your friends drive you nuts, blah blah blah. Or maybe you just have a bad attitude and like it that way. Fair enough—raining on other people's parades *can* be fun. But do you actually *like* being sick, sleep deprived, and friendless? Of course not, you weirdo. So use this guided journal to help you embrace the suck, but also to help you look on the bright side, turn your frown upside down, make raindrops into rainbows…and maybe, just maybe, start to feel some freaking happiness in spite of yourself.

Okay, you bought this book, which probably means you've got a bad attitude but are a *little* (teeny, tiny) bit open to changing it. Let's start with identifying just how negative you really are.

Did you know that naming your bad feelings actually makes them less intense? It's f*cking science, so you can't argue with it. Think about all the crap in your life that's bringing you down. How do those thoughts make you feel?

Use the checklist below to identify your negative emotions. Use the blank lines to write in any that are missing from the list.

Unhappy

Awkward

Irritated

Stressed

Tired

Angry

Tense

Blah

Anxious

Lonely

Frustrated

Offended

Ambivalent

◯ Regretful of spending money on this stupid book

Cranky

Uncertain

Worried

◯ Checklists are bullsh*t

◯ _____

LOOK BACK

at what you checked off on the previous page. Is there one emotion that you're feeling more strongly than the others? Or that you feel more frequently than the others? Yeah, it's hard to pick just one of your crappy feelings to focus on, but do it anyway.

Use the space here to explain what's behind that feeling. Is there a specific event that's triggered you, or does something happen regularly that sets you off? Is the feeling tied to some idiot person? To a place? Or are there are a million sh*tty little things conspiring against you? Whatever the reason(s), now's your chance to get it all out.

I feel _____ *because*

_____

_____

_____

_____

_____

_____

_____

_____

_____

_____

Now it's time for some

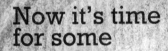

GRATITUDE

(You didn't think you'd just get to *complain* the whole time, did you? WTH, aren't you whiny enough already?) Turn your attention to some things that are going well in your life. Don't be dramatic—you can think of *something* if you try hard enough. Think of everything positive, even if it seems minor.

Now how do you feel?

Use the checklist below to identify your positive emotions. Use the blank lines to write in any that are missing from the list.

- ○ Positive thinking is hard
- ○ Happy
- ○ Content
- ○ Appreciative
- ○ Calm
- ○ Blessed
- ○ Energized
- ○ Relaxed
- ○ Inspired
- ○ Excited
- ○ Curious

- ○ Satisfied
- ○ Determined
- ○ Proud
- ○ Cheerful
- ○ Serene
- ○ Motivated
- ○ Checklists are still bullsh*t
- ○ _____
- ○ _____
- ○ _____
- ○ _____

Look back at what you checked off on the previous page. It's probably a longer list than you thought it would be, isn't it? Maybe you're not as angsty as you thought you were!

Which of those positive emotions are you most surprised to recognize in yourself? What do you think is behind it? Are you glad to be feeling that way, or does it feel unusual because you're used to being such a freaking downer about everything? Use the space here to explore where this positive emotion is coming from—and what you could do to enhance it.

(Yep, enhance!)

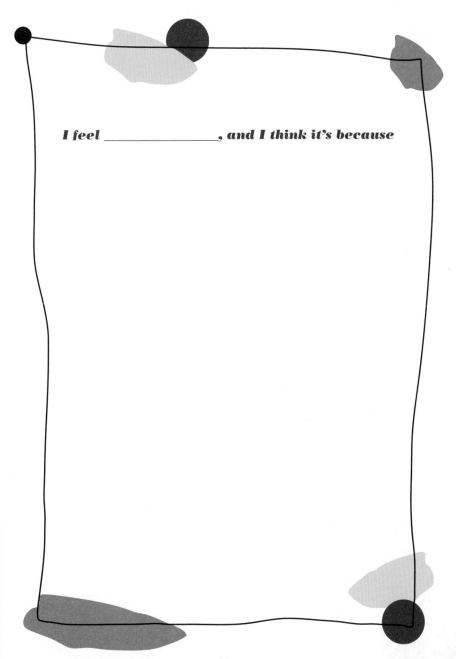

I feel _____, and I think it's because

SCRIBBLE BREAK!

Grab markers, colored pencils, or crayons in a variety of your favorite colors and use them to scribble all over these pages. The act of scribbling will channel your inner destructo, but the result will be beautiful. It's a win-win!

"Whether you think you can, or you think you can't— you're right."

—Henry Ford

Have you ever expected the worst of a situation, and then it was just as lame as you'd thought?

On the flip side, have you managed to psych yourself up about rocking something nerve-racking...and then you did totally rock it? Don't get cocky—it's not like you have magical powers or something. But your thinking *can* guide your behavior. It's not just woo-woo, New Age-y bullsh*t: psychology confirms it! Imagining a positive outcome can actually help lead to a positive outcome.

Put your imagination to work and use the space below to bring something positive into your future.

I'm worried about _____.

The positive outcome I visualize is:

TRY NOT TO *think of a* UNICORN!

(It's impossible, right? Now all you can think about is a unicorn—and you're **way too cool** to be thinking about some stupid, trendy-ass unicorn.)

The more you try to suppress a thought, the more you end up obsessing over it. Don't worry, you're not suddenly OCD. This is a real psychological phenomenon ("ironic process theory," in case you're a geek), and the bottom line is this: your brain is being an asshole.

Want to know how to stop thinking about that thing? Ironically, the trick is **intentionally** thinking about it *in a way that you control.* So what is your f*cking unicorn? Maybe something happened to make you feel embarrassed, or guilty, or sad, or whatever...and it keeps popping up no matter how much you try to distract yourself. Use the space below to write about it, on your own terms.

_____

_____

_____

_____

_____

Another way to counteract the unicorn? Pick a specific distractor to think about instead. Maybe something positive, like, I dunno... something you're **grateful** for? Every time the unicorn pops up, switch to your gratitude thought—you'll be thinking happier, less obsessive thoughts in no time.

I am replacing my unicorn with:

_____

_____

_____

_____

_____

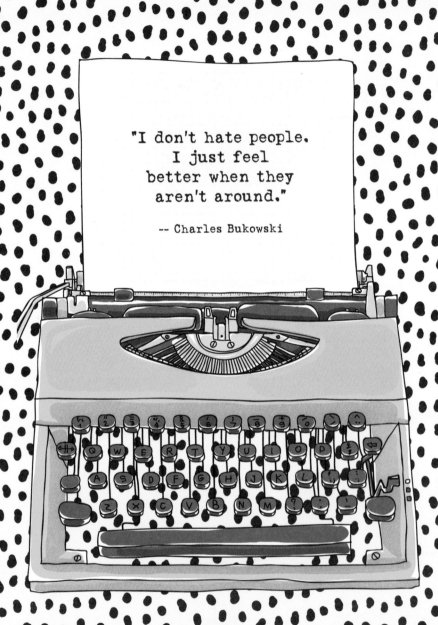

"I don't hate people.
I just feel
better when they
aren't around."

-- Charles Bukowski

You don't have to be a full-on misanthrope to need some alone time at least occasionally. Some people call this "self-care," others call it "recharging"... others call it being lazy or boring. Who f*cking cares? You need it, so embrace it. What does quality **you time** look like? A solitary hike? A pants-free Netflix binge? A candlelit bubble bath, like you're a character in some cheesy Hallmark Channel movie? (No judgment!) Draw a picture of it in the space below.

When was the last time
you indulged yourself
in this alone time?
If it's been a while,
plan some now!

little *things*
ADD UP

It's way too easy to get distracted by irritations and frustrations—some days, *everything* gets on your nerves, and it all accumulates to turn you into a fire-breathing monster. It's much, much harder to let minor joys and comforts add up and put you in a good mood, isn't it?

Just like a million small irritations can add up to make you hate the world, small pleasures can add up to put you in a decent mood, if you'd actually let them. Spend the next week paying attention to the little things. Depending on how sunny your disposition *isn't*, it may feel unnatural to focus on positive things—but it will get easier if you try!

What's irritating you? But more important, what's making you happy? How do they balance out? See if you notice any change in your mood or outlook by the end of the week.

	What bugged you?	What brought you joy?	How do you feel today?
Day 1			
Day 2			
Day 3			
Day 4			
Day 5			
Day 6			
Day 7			

NOPE
NOPE
NOPE
NOPE

"NO"

is usually a negative word—but TBH, it can be really positive when it's used to cut bullsh*t from your life. We all end up saying "yes" to things we shouldn't...either out of guilt, out of obligation, because we're doormats, or just because we're not clever enough to come up with a good excuse. But saying "yes" all the time can suck your energy and get you stuck spending time on things that aren't important to you.

What are some things you need to start saying "no" to more often?

1. _____

2. _____

3. _____

4. _____

5. _____

Now put this into practice and spend a few days saying "no" to all the requests that come your way. *How does it feel to finally enforce some freaking boundaries?*

_____

_____

_____

_____

_____

"There are more tears shed over answered prayers than over unanswered prayers."

—Saint Teresa of Avila

Does it seem like everybody else is chasing after a bunch of insane goals that sound like way more work than they're worth, while you're proud of yourself just for getting your dishes washed and your teeth brushed? A negative person might call that "being lazy." But you? You're a (kind of) positive person by this point, right? A positive person calls that "being content with what you have."

Use each of the circles to write an annoying life goal you have no interest in achieving. When you're done, take a red pencil or marker and draw a giant X through each. WTG!

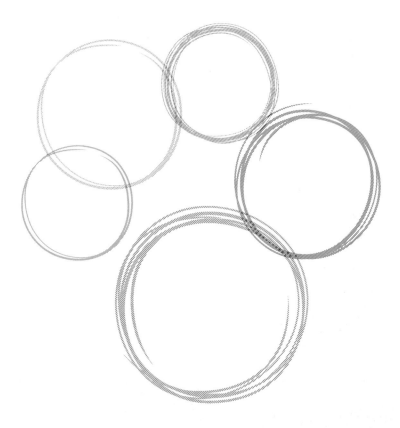

A BAD MOOD DOESN'T HAVE TO BE A NEGATIVE THING IF YOU ENJOY IT.

"But wait," you might be asking. "Is it really a **bad** mood if it actually makes you feel **good**?" Well aren't you f*cking clever.

Sometimes you just want to wallow. So what do you turn to when you want to indulge in a bad mood? Comfort food? A crying jag? Something productive, like an intense workout? Or something destructive, like texting your ex?

Use this space to draw a picture of what it looks like when you have your **BEST. BAD MOOD. EVER.**

Refer back to it next time you're feeling sad/angry/cranky/blah and have no interest in turning things around.

Not all bad moods are created equal, **and sometimes even YOU need cheering up.**

Face it: no matter how much you enjoy being your own living, breathing storm cloud, sometimes you need the rain to stop so you can feel the sun.

What do you do to cheer yourself up when you need it? Listen to music? OD on carbs? Look at pics of cute puppies on the internet? Or something destructive, like online stalking your ex? (Hey, it works for some people...) Use this space to draw a picture of the most effective way you have of cheering yourself up, and refer back to it later on the off-chance that you need it.

"There is nothing either good or bad, but thinking makes it so."

— *Hamlet*, William Shakespeare

*Sometimes good things happen, and sometimes sh*tty things happen.*

Other times, things happen that we *think* are sh*tty, but only because we're approaching them from our usual sh*tty perspective. What seems like the end of the world can actually be a lesson learned; a missed opportunity can position us for an even better opportunity.

(Whoa, what if silver linings *are a real thing*? **Mind blown.**)

Think of something that happened in your past that felt sh*tty at the time, but that turned out not so bad. Now think of a sh*tty thing that's happened lately. Describe it here:

_____

_____

_____

_____

_____

Now turn the situation on its head. What's something positive that came/will come out of it?

_____

_____

_____

_____

_____

DESCRIBE YOUR FAVORITES!

1. _____

_____

_____

_____

2. _____

_____

_____

_____

3. _____

_____

_____

_____

Ever get a song stuck in your head
and it won't go away and it

DRIVES.
YOU.
CRAZY?

Ugh! Music is powerful stuff, and it's
amazing how it can influence our
moods—in both good and **terrible**
ways. The right song at the right time
can make your soul soar…and the
wrong song can make it sore. (Even
more sore than bad puns…)

What songs make you want to gouge out your eardrums?

1. _____
2. _____
3. _____
4. _____
5. _____

What songs make you feel like a rock star/diva/karaoke champ?

1. _____
2. _____
3. _____
4. _____
5. _____

Go make a playlist of your favorites right now!
Listen to it next time you need a pick-me-up.

WHERE DOES ALL YOUR FREE TIME GO?

Probably not to stuff you truly enjoy. Work and showering and other necessary forms of adulting are one thing, but your free time should be your own...right? So think about where your time is actually going, and whether you're OK with that. How much do you spend with people you don't even like that much? Just how many waking hours do you spend mindlessly scrolling through your phone, or binging Netflix shows you're not that into?

Use this space to create a pie chart illustrating how you divide your time. Be honest with yourself.

Now think about what you'd rather be doing with your time—you probably wish you were more focused on things that are important to you.

Maybe that's self-improvement, like working out or writing short stories; maybe it's spending more time with friends and family. Or hell, maybe it's spending *less* time with friends and family and more time drinking alone. You do you. Think about what you can do to get more in control of your own time and achieve the balance you've been craving.

Use this space to create a pie chart of where your time should be going, in your ideal world.

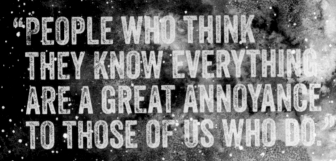

"PEOPLE WHO THINK
THEY KNOW EVERYTHING
ARE A GREAT ANNOYANCE
TO THOSE OF US WHO DO."

—ISAAC ASIMOV

One problem with other people is that so many of them are just so dumb, aren't they? Not you, of course—you're brilliant, and you know it. Maybe you don't know *everything*, but you definitely know a lot about *something*. So prove it here. What's something you're an expert at? Where do you excel? Write about or draw a picture of it here. ***Show off a little!***

Stay the f*ck out of my bubble.

Draw yourself in the center bubble. In the smaller bubbles, surround yourself with people you actually like: family members, friends, significant other, even your pets. Don't include any toxic people in your life—those mother*ckers need to stay out of your bubble.

SOCIAL MEDIA DETOX

Whether it's Facebook, Instagram, Snapchat, Twitter…admit it, regardless of your social media drug of choice, you're totally addicted. And what do you mostly do on there? Get annoyed with how dumb other people are, and make yourself feel like sh*t because you're constantly comparing your life to other people's. What are the things that drive you nuts online?

1. _____

2. _____

3. _____

4. _____

5. _____

Seriously, don't you have more productive and mentally healthy things you could be doing? Make a list of things you can do instead of wasting time scrolling through social media, and refer back to it next time you get the itch.

1. _____

2. _____

3. _____

4. _____

5. _____

"We hate it when our friends become successful."

—MORRISSEY

You love your friends. But it's SO annoying when good things happen to them instead of to you. Whether it's a promotion, a hot date, or more "likes" on a status update, sometimes good things happen to the wrong people. And even if we're happy for our friends, sometimes we're also **jealous**.

When did something great happen to a loved one, and you had to put on a happy face even though you were dying inside?

_____

_____

_____

_____

_____

_____

_____

_____

_____

Moment of Zen

Feeling overwhelmed by all the thoughts swirling around your brain, and need to calm your mind? Coloring is a great way to relieve stress! It promotes "mindfulness" and "flow" and a bunch of other crap that's supposed to relax you. So use some colorful pens or pencils and fill in the image on the opposite page: choose soothing shades, create a beautiful pattern, and you'll be in a blissful state of serenity by the time you're through.

Moment of

You know what's another good way to relieve stress? Taking your anger out on an inanimate object by scribbling your ass off! Forget about staying within the lines—they're not the boss of you! Find a black marker or crayon and surrender to your rage by scribbling as hard and fast as you can all across the page. By the time you've made the paper as dark as your mood, you'll also have exhausted yourself.

Don't you feel better?

Treat

You spend so much of your time
putting up with other people and
their bullsh*t—you deserve a
reward! What are the ways that you
reward yourself when you're proud
of your accomplishments…or just
proud of yourself for not yelling
at anybody stupid today? Draw
pictures of yo' favorite treats here.

yo' self!

Be yourself, and if other people don't like it, f*ck them.

We all have annoying qualities and habits (yes, even *you*). Some of us embrace our quirks, and others are insecure about them because we're afraid of people thinking we're annoying. You probably spend a lot of time and effort trying to keep that sh*t in check because you're worried other people won't like you.

Guess what?

Some people aren't going to like you anyway! But who cares?
Those b*tches are lame. So what have you been holding
back? What makes you uniquely *you*? Draw a picture or write
about it below.

Some people say that living well is the best revenge. But some of us disagree:

STRAIGHT-UP REVENGE IS THE BEST REVENGE.

The problem is, revenge isn't always practical…or legal… But that doesn't mean you can't still fantasize about it. Think of someone who pissed you the f*ck off or did something mean to you. You can't actually execute it, but you can use this space to write about or draw your darkest revenge scenario. Laxatives? Prank call to a SWAT team? LEGOs left on the floor in the dark? Go nuts, you lunatic.

GET over IT

As fun as it is to plot revenge, stewing over how somebody else wronged you—especially when there's nothing you can do about it—will only make YOU feel more angry and bitter. And what good does that do you; aren't you angry and bitter enough already? Sometimes you just need to freaking let it go.

*What's something you've been holding on to for too long? What do you need to do to get the f*ck over it?*

NO FILTER!

Being polite sucks when you're dealing with assholes you have to pretend to like. Whether you're putting up with your boss, your roommate, or your crazy uncle, you've had to bite your tongue more than once just to keep the peace.

Break your silence!
Fill in these speech bubbles with what's *really* on your mind.

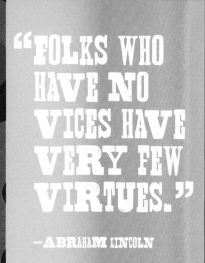

"FOLKS WHO HAVE NO VICES HAVE VERY FEW VIRTUES."

—ABRAHAM LINCOLN

60

Lincoln was called "Honest Abe" for a reason—so you know he's not lying about how lame it is to have no vices. Being well behaved is fine and all, but not if it makes you a goody-goody.

VICES ARE THE BEST! WRITE ABOUT YOUR FAVORITES HERE.

Vice: _____

I f*cking love this because _____

_____

_____

_____

_____

Vice: _____

I f*cking love this because _____

_____

_____

_____

_____

Vice: _____

I f*cking love this because _____

_____

_____

_____

_____

DELAYED BRILLIANCE IS THE F*CKING WORST.

Oh, snap! Ever get into it with someone and come up with a killer retort…but not until hours after the fact, when you're replaying the argument in your head? Finally get your flirt on with the hottie you've been eyeing for weeks, sound like a moron in the moment, but then think of the perfect witty response *days* later? Use these pages to let yourself shine: re-create the scene, but with your perfect comeback.

Some people are like
clouds: they disappear
and the day gets

BRIGHTER.

You have at least one person in your life who is a big ol' toxic storm cloud rolling in to darken your day. What makes this person such a downer?

_____

_____

_____

_____

_____

What can you do to avoid encountering this asshole? If interactions are inevitable, what can you do to minimize the toxicity so you can feel a little sunlight?

_____

_____

_____

_____

_____

Coloring break!

Fill in this pattern with your favorite colors. It's relaxing and sh*t.

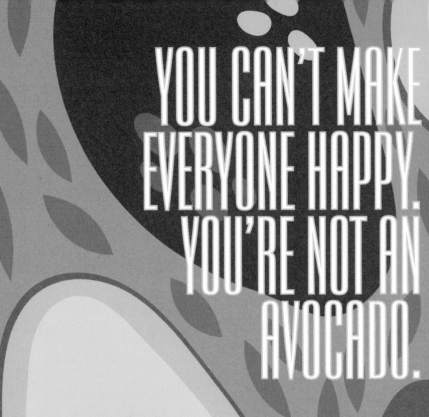

YOU CAN'T MAKE EVERYONE HAPPY. YOU'RE NOT AN AVOCADO.

Are you a people pleaser? Maybe that explains why you're such a miserable ass. Because there are two big problems with trying to make everybody else happy all the time:
1) It's impossible.
2) You end up sacrificing *your own* happiness in the process.

So being a people pleaser is f*cking dumb.

What are some ways that you're trying to please everybody else? How would you make YOURSELF feel better if you stopped?

_____

_____

_____

_____

_____

_____

_____

_____

_____

I'M NO CACTUS EXPERT, BUT I KNOW A PRICK WHEN I SEE ONE.

You probably know a prick, too (or several). Use this space to complain about this person. Don't worry about coming across as a prick yourself—this is a safe space.

_____

_____

_____

_____

_____

_____

_____

_____

_____

_____

TAKE
THIS
JOB
AND
SHOVE
IT

Fact: unless you're a trust-fund baby or a superstar Instagram influencer, you're a loser who has to work for a living just like every other schmuck. Another fact: work sucks, and you'd quit tomorrow if you could—even if you love your job, you've fantasized about bailing.

Use the space here to write about or illustrate your most dramatic, epic exit fantasy.

Somebody else's therapist knows all about you.

Not that you're the reason that person is in therapy, but…you've probably really f*cked up someone else's head at some point. Whether you tormented your younger sibling, went a teensy bit psycho during a breakup, or lost your sh*t with an annoying coworker—chances are, somebody out there has some serious beef with you. Use the space below to describe your behavior. Are you embarrassed about it, or proud of it? (Probably proud. You asshole.)

_____

_____

_____

_____

_____

_____

_____

_____

_____

_____

DON'T FORGET TO YELL "JENGA!" AS YOUR LIFE FALLS APART!

Doing nothing can be rad—that's what Netflix binges and boozy brunches were made for, right? But doing nothing is also a great way to screw yourself if you have goals you want to accomplish or sh*t you just need to get done. Admit it, you've got *something* on your to-do list that needs to be crossed off before it screws up your life even more, whether it's unf*cking your finances or just tackling your disgusting bathroom. You haven't started doing it yet because you're lazy or because you're overwhelmed (or both).

Breaking your big task
down into manageable
steps will help you feel
less intimidated and start
making some freaking
progress. Use the boxes here to build
a PLAN. Each box represents
a step you need to take; add
those steps up, and you'll have
accomplished what you need
to accomplish in no time.
After you've put your plan
together, get off your ass
and get started!

"IF YOU GIVE UP ON YOUR DREAMS, WHAT'S LEFT?"

—Jim Carrey

What's a dream or goal you have that you don't think you'll ever reach? Maybe you're too lazy, too incompetent, or too unmotivated to achieve it— or maybe, if you're honest with yourself, *you don't care about it that much anymore*. Sometimes we get so hooked on *pursuing* a goal that we stop even thinking about whether the end result is still important to us. If you gave up a dream, you might be left with nothing...or you might be left with the time, passion, and energy to pursue a *new* dream that you're actually excited about.

The dream I want to give up on is _____

By giving it up, I'll gain:
1. _____
2. _____
3. _____
4. _____
5. _____

You shouldn't give up on *all* your dreams, though. What's a dream you're still excited about?

_____

What will you gain by achieving it?
1. _____
2. _____
3. _____
4. _____
5. _____

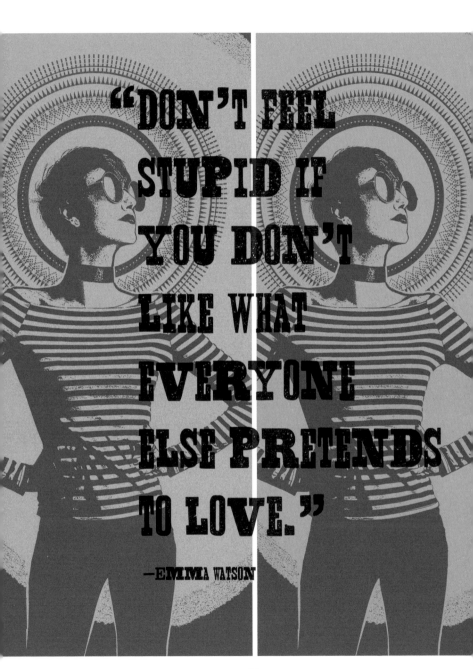

"DON'T FEEL STUPID IF YOU DON'T LIKE WHAT EVERYONE ELSE PRETENDS TO LOVE."

—EMMA WATSON

What are some things everybody else is obsessed with that you despise? Whether you hate a hit song, a fashion fad, or even a major movie franchise that won't seem to die, you don't have to feel like a loser for not being into what everybody else is into—sometimes what's trendy is SUPER F*CKING LAME. Drawing pictures or using your words, use the space below to describe something popular that you just can't stand.

Let your freak flag fly!

Now celebrate the things you love, whether they're popular or not. What are some of the hobbies, interests, and obsessions that make you unique?

emotional sniffles

Ever find yourself around somebody who's coughing
and sneezing all over the place (gross!), and, despite
your best efforts to avoid contact, within a day or two
you've got their nasty bug too? Likewise, ever find
yourself in a good mood, then get around your Debbie
Downer coworker or your sourpuss roommate...and
within an hour, your good mood has drained away?
Feelings are like colds: inconvenient and contagious.
You can "catch" emotions—negative and positive—
from the people around you.

Feeling cranky? What do you do that infects the people around you?

_____

_____

_____

_____

_____

Feeling positive? How can you spread that to others?

_____

_____

_____

_____

_____

Stuck in a rut? No wonder you feel lousy, you loser.

What's a habit you need to break? You probably have a few. Maybe you skipped the gym in favor of Taco Tuesday, and it turned into Taco Wednesday, and Taco Thursday, and then Taco Friday…Maybe you keep going back to your jerk-face ex just because it's familiar. Maybe you just never make yourself go to bed at a decent hour.

Your routine plays a **huge** role in your emotional state and whether you feel good or bad on a daily basis. Explore what bad habit you need to break and how it would help you, then think of a good habit you need to start enforcing and why.

Bad habit:

_____

_____

_____

_____

_____

Good habit:

_____

_____

_____

_____

_____

It's OK to hate—but it's not cool to hate on yourself.

Think of some of the worst things you've said to yourself. Would you let somebody else talk to you like that? Of course not. You'd cut that b*tch.

Take each mean thing you think or say about yourself, and flip it on its head. It might be hard to give yourself a compliment, but you deserve it! (Seriously!)

Self, you suck because _____

_____

But you're actually awesome because _____

_____

I get mad at myself sometimes because _____

_____

But then I totally redeem myself by _____

_____

Self, you suck because _____

_____

But you're actually awesome because _____

_____

I get mad at myself sometimes because _____

_____

But then I totally redeem myself by _____

_____

I FEEL SO MISERABLE WITHOUT YOU, IT'S ALMOST LIKE HAVING YOU HERE.

Your loved ones: sometimes YOU JUST CAN'T EVEN.
Whether it's your needy best friend or your super-
judgy-about-your-lifestyle-choices mom, chances are
there's someone close to you who's been annoying AF
lately. Make a list of the things that have been driving
you crazy about this person. (It's OK, nobody has to
know but you.)

1. ⁓⁓⁓⁓⁓⁓⁓⁓⁓⁓⁓⁓⁓⁓⁓⁓⁓⁓⁓⁓⁓⁓⁓⁓⁓⁓⁓⁓⁓⁓
2. ⁓⁓⁓⁓⁓⁓⁓⁓⁓⁓⁓⁓⁓⁓⁓⁓⁓⁓⁓⁓⁓⁓⁓⁓⁓⁓⁓⁓⁓⁓
3. ⁓⁓⁓⁓⁓⁓⁓⁓⁓⁓⁓⁓⁓⁓⁓⁓⁓⁓⁓⁓⁓⁓⁓⁓⁓⁓⁓⁓⁓⁓
4. ⁓⁓⁓⁓⁓⁓⁓⁓⁓⁓⁓⁓⁓⁓⁓⁓⁓⁓⁓⁓⁓⁓⁓⁓⁓⁓⁓⁓⁓⁓
5. ⁓⁓⁓⁓⁓⁓⁓⁓⁓⁓⁓⁓⁓⁓⁓⁓⁓⁓⁓⁓⁓⁓⁓⁓⁓⁓⁓⁓⁓⁓

But let's be real: even when your loved ones are
being assholes, you still love them and need them in
your life. Feeling bad because you complained about
that person above? Assuage your guilt and balance
your karma by reminding yourself of what you love
most about them. (And when you're done, go remind
them, too—it won't kill you to show a little gratitude,
you know.)

1. ⁓⁓⁓⁓⁓⁓⁓⁓⁓⁓⁓⁓⁓⁓⁓⁓⁓⁓⁓⁓⁓⁓⁓⁓⁓⁓⁓⁓⁓⁓
2. ⁓⁓⁓⁓⁓⁓⁓⁓⁓⁓⁓⁓⁓⁓⁓⁓⁓⁓⁓⁓⁓⁓⁓⁓⁓⁓⁓⁓⁓⁓
3. ⁓⁓⁓⁓⁓⁓⁓⁓⁓⁓⁓⁓⁓⁓⁓⁓⁓⁓⁓⁓⁓⁓⁓⁓⁓⁓⁓⁓⁓⁓
4. ⁓⁓⁓⁓⁓⁓⁓⁓⁓⁓⁓⁓⁓⁓⁓⁓⁓⁓⁓⁓⁓⁓⁓⁓⁓⁓⁓⁓⁓⁓
5. ⁓⁓⁓⁓⁓⁓⁓⁓⁓⁓⁓⁓⁓⁓⁓⁓⁓⁓⁓⁓⁓⁓⁓⁓⁓⁓⁓⁓⁓⁓

BEING A GRUMPY
CAT IS ONE THING...
BEING A SCAREDY-
CAT IS ANOTHER.

You probably let fear hold you back from doing things you really want to do. Whether it's applying for a promotion, asking somebody on a date, or just learning how to do your own laundry, you probably psych yourself out because you anticipate disaster. Guess what, you big baby: the worst possible outcome is never as bad as you imagine, and you'll survive just fine. Guess what else? Being afraid is just going to leave you with a lot of unfulfilled dreams and a whole sh*t-ton of regret.

What's something you're being a scaredy-cat about?

_____

_____

_____

_____

_____

What's the worst that can happen, *really?* Is it going to kill you?

_____

_____

_____

_____

_____

HATERS GONNA HATE.

AND SOMETIMES THE HATER IS YOU.

Make a list of things you hate. Go ahead, embrace it. You know you want to.

1. _____
2. _____
3. _____
4. _____
5. _____
6. _____
7. _____
8. _____
9. _____
10. _____
11. _____
12. _____
13. _____
14. _____
15. _____
16. _____
17. _____
18. _____
19. _____
20. _____

Love ♥ & Hate

Now think of things you love. It's OK to admit you love things, it's not going to ruin your street cred. (Refer back to your previous list if you need to… because maybe what you love is being a hater? And there's no shame in that.)

Make a list of things you love.

1. _____
2. _____
3. _____
4. _____
5. _____
6. _____
7. _____
8. _____
9. _____
10. _____
11. _____
12. _____
13. _____
14. _____
15. _____
16. _____
17. _____
18. _____
19. _____
20. _____

Gratitude is about being thankful for the positive things in life, and sometimes those positive things are BIG ones. A new job, an amazing vacation, an engagement, or some other major life event...these things deserve celebrating!

But let's be real: part of the fun is posting about the big thing on social media so you can bask in the glow of "likes" and heart emojis, knowing each one represents someone else's raging case of FOMO.

Don't lie, you know it feels good to make other people a little jealous sometimes.

What's a FOMO-inducing thing that you've done? How did other people's responses make you feel?

Now imagine nobody else gave a sh*t about your thing. That wouldn't actually make it any less great, would it? Write about how awesome the thing was in and of itself.

_____

_____

_____

_____

_____

_____

_____

_____

_____

Light
as a
Feather

You probably have A LOT of worries—
some of them legitimate, others not, and all of
them weighing you the f*ck down. What if
you could eliminate them? Write one of your
troubles on each of the feathers here, and
metaphorically blow them all away!

Admit it, you judge other people ALL THE TIME. Guess what? Whether you like it or not, those assholes are judging you right back. Use this space to explore the judgments you think (or know) other people have about you.

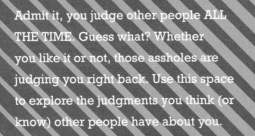

Write out each judgment on these pages. If something bothers you, make a note about what you can do to change it. If something doesn't bother you, cross it out and vow never to give a sh*t.

color page

to reflect your mood
RIGHT NOW.

Feeling foul?
Use black, blues,
and grays.

Feeling pretty f*cking
spectacular? Use
the brightest colors
you can stand.

LET THE
HATE FLOW
THROUGH YOU.

Use this space for stream of consciousness—
write about whatever is pissing you the f*ck
off at the moment. Put down whatever comes
to mind, uncensored!

_____

_____

_____

_____

_____

_____

_____

_____

_____

_____

_____

_____

_____

SALTY AND SWEET

It applies to the best snacks…and probably also applies
to you, doesn't it? Admit it, you're kinda irritating sometimes.
But you're a big old sweetie, too, aren't you? It's the perfect
combo, so embrace it. Use this space to celebrate what makes
you salty, AND what makes you sweet.

Salty:

_____

_____

_____

_____

_____

Sweet:

_____

_____

_____

_____

_____

If you're not

GRATEFUL

*for what you already have, what makes
you think you'd be happy with more?*

It doesn't matter how cranky, bitter, pissed off, negative, or irritated you are—*you have things to be grateful for, and the only path toward happiness is embracing those things.* Use the space here to draw pictures of or write about the things you're grateful for. And continue converting your "grrr-atitude" to genuine **gratitude** every f*cking day.

IMAGE CREDITS

Page 1: iStock/vector (lightning bolt), DigitalVision Vectors/RENGraphic (rainbow) • page 2: iStock/enjoynz • pages 3, 111: iStock/VectorFun • page 4: iStock/Vaselena • pages 6–7: iStock/mymny • pages 8–9: iStock/Hulinska_Yevheniia • pages 10–11: iStock/Benjavisa • page 12: iStock/chaluk • pages 14–15: iStock/beastfromeast • pages 16–17: iStock/DrAfter123 • pages 18, 112: iStock/quisp65 • pages 20–21: iStock/gmm2000 (typewriter), dartlab (dots) • page 22: Stockio.com • page 24: Stockio.com • pages 26–27: iStock/Suriko (eyes), filo (circles) • pages 28-29: iStock/Sky_melody • pages 30–31: iStock/invincible_bulldog • page 32: Stockio.com • page 34: iStock/Beeldbewerking • pages 36–37: iStock/ArtLana • pages 38–39: iStock/ilyast • page 40: iStock/Nebula Cordata • pages 42–43: iStock/AlexandrMoroz • pages 44–45: iStock/ exdez • pages 46–47: iStock/beastfromeast • pages 48–49: iStock/hudiemm (scribble), IgorKrapar (type), Alka5051 (paisley) • pages 50–51: iStock/VikiVector • pages 54–55: iStock/FrankRamspott • pages 56–57: Stockio.com • pages 58–59: iStock/pijama61 • page 60: iStock/CSA-Printstock (Lincoln), shellpreast (background) • pages 62–63: iStock/beastfromeast • page 64: iStock/ass29 • pages 66–67: iStock/elfiny (scribble), hudiemm (cactus illustration) • page 68: iStock/Anna Sidorova • page 70: iStock/dianne555 • page 72: iStock/cosmaa • page 74: iStock/lemonadeserendae • page 78: iStock/beastfromeast • page 80: iStock/GeorgePeters • pages 82–83: iStock/nidwlw • page 84: iStock/ourlifelooklikeballoon (tissue box), andipantz (background) • pages 86–87: iStock/nezezon2 • pages 88–89 iStock/wissanu99 (reflection), Nalaleana (frame) • pages 90–91: iStock/VectorFun (cat), ToriArt (circles) • pages 92–93: iStock/stevenfoley • pages 94, 96: iStock/Suriyub • pages 98–99: iStock/Illerlok_Xolms • pages 100–101: iStock/saemilee • page 102: iStock/zak00 • pages 104–105: iStock/linaflerova • page 106: iStock/d3images • pages 108–109: iStock/ioanmasay • pages 110–111: Stockio.com (flower), iStock/nezezon2 (taco), beastfromeast (lemon & llama), VikiVector (donut), treehouse (pug), JohnWrightman (cactus)